BELONGS TO :

____

1

TERRICKA HARDY, LCSW, ACSW, BCD

Copyright © 2020 Terricka Hardy
All Rights Reserved
ISBN: 9798662881815

About Color Out Loud ™ for #SocialWorkers

Dear #SocialWorkers, YOU ROCK!

Being a Social Worker is challenging all by itself, yet it is rewarding. Let's face it, there are just some things that we experience that others do not. *Color Out Loud ™ for #SocialWorkers* was created for social workers by a social worker. It is a safe space and self-care tool for you to give voice to your thoughts. The average person has nearly 60,000 thoughts per day, yet we are rarely aware of them due to the demands of work and life. *Color Out Loud ™ for #SocialWorkers* affords you the opportunity to make space for those funny yet practice related thoughts you often think but rarely say out loud. Laugh & Color Out Loud ™ as you enjoy the gift of humor and give personality to your thoughts. Let's Color Out Loud ™!

How to use this book

There are NO RULES. This book includes various practice related phrases and truths for #SocialWorkers. They were created to promote self-awareness and some to literally make you laugh out loud. Here are a few tips to help you get started:

1. Find a phrase that resonates with you.
2. Read the phrase out loud.
3. Think about why and how this phrase resonates most with you. Then reflect on the phrase and laugh out loud, even.
4. Color Away!
5. Have a colleague to join you. You'll enjoy the process even more! Grab a copy of this book for a colleague and enjoy!

4

I'M THE CLOSEST YOU'LL EVER GET TO A SUPERHERO!
#SOCIALWORKER

I'M KIND OF
A BIG DEAL!
#BOMBSOCIALWORKER

I'm a social worker, nothing surprises me.
#I'veSeenItAll

7

My clients are better than yours.
#rapport

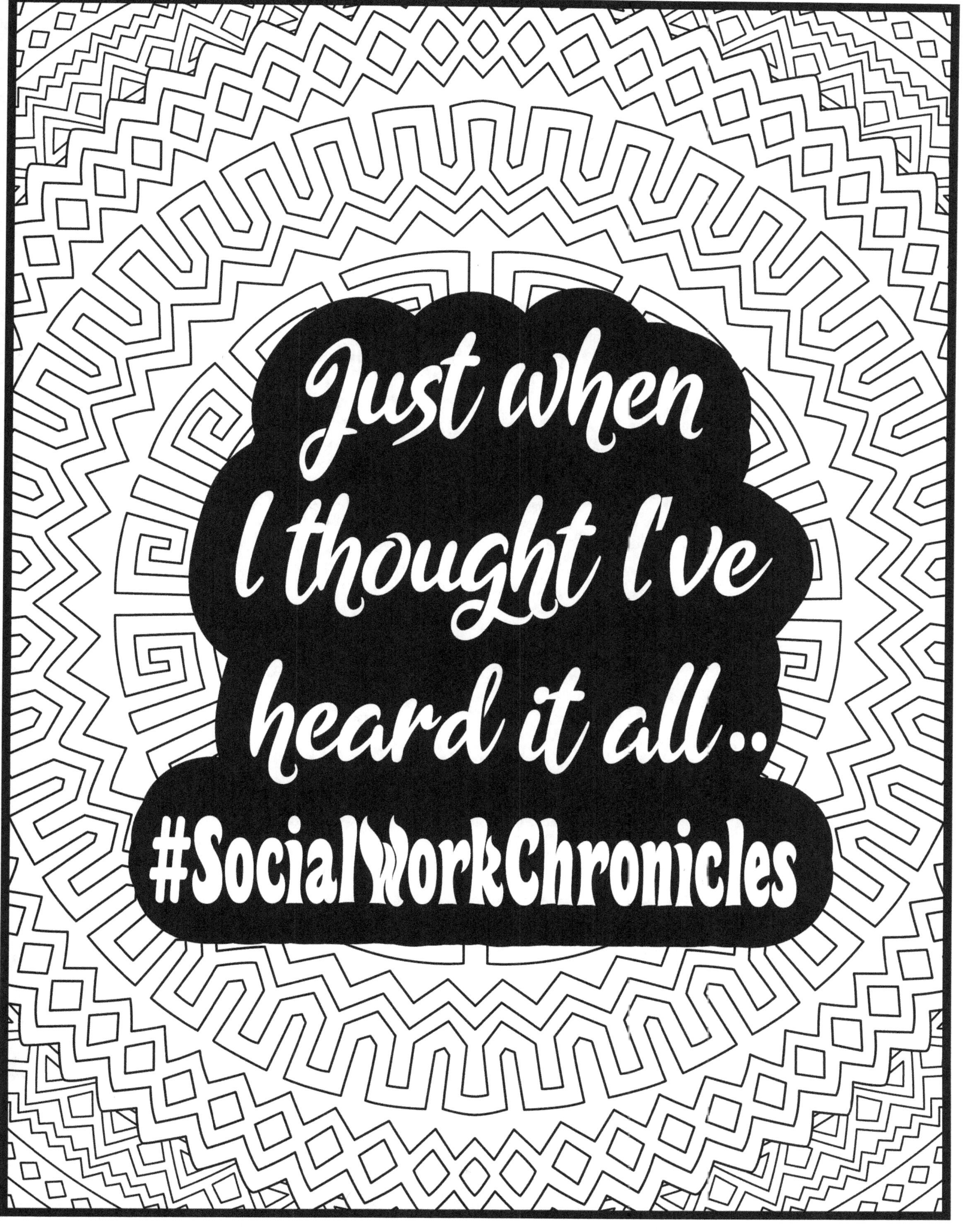

Just when I thought I've heard it all..
#SocialWorkChronicles

9

PTO me,
Please!
#self-care

TODAY,
I CHOOSE
SELF-CARE.
#IT'SMYDAYOFF

11

Change
Agent
#BeTheChange

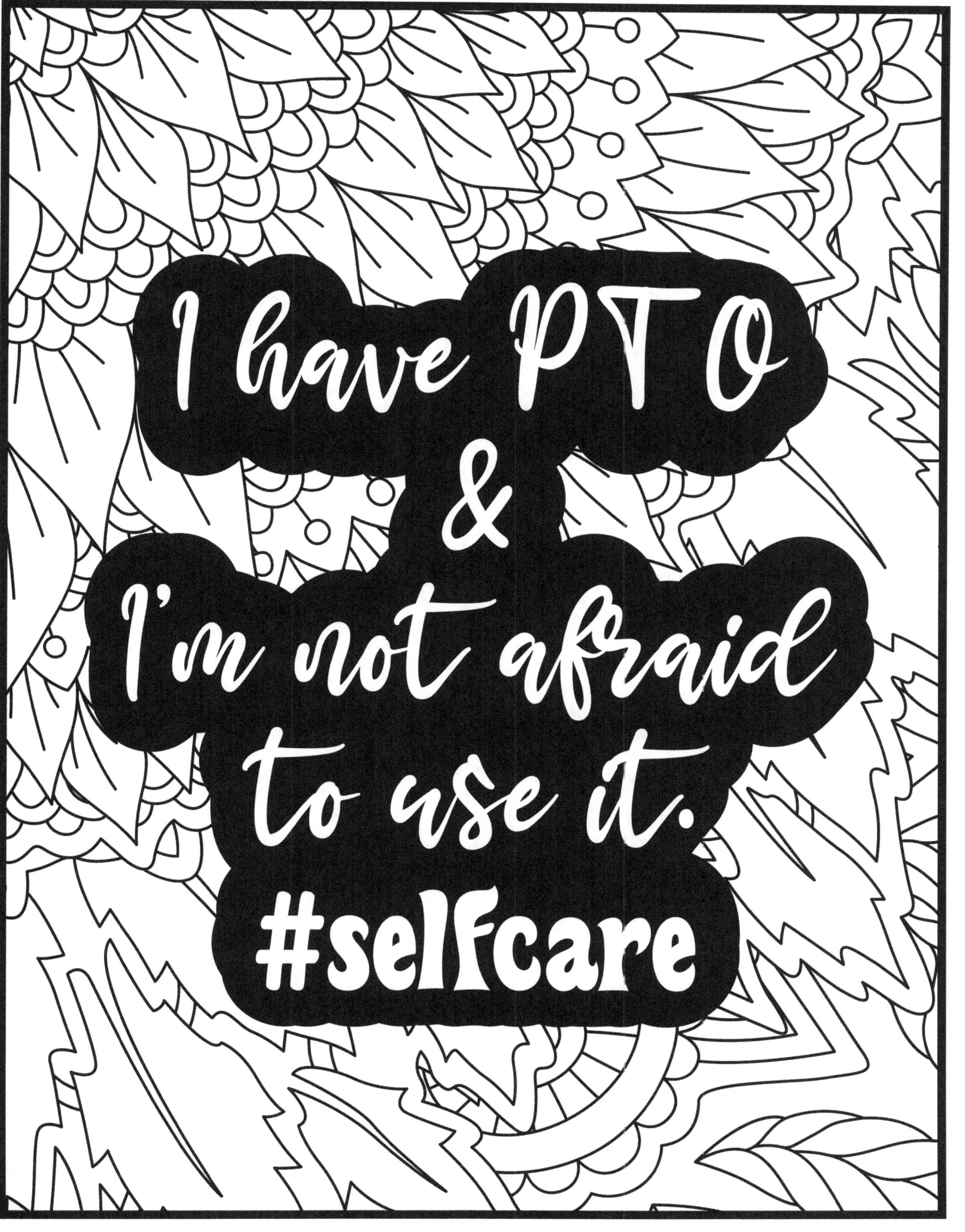

I have PTO
&
I'm not afraid
to use it.
#selfcare

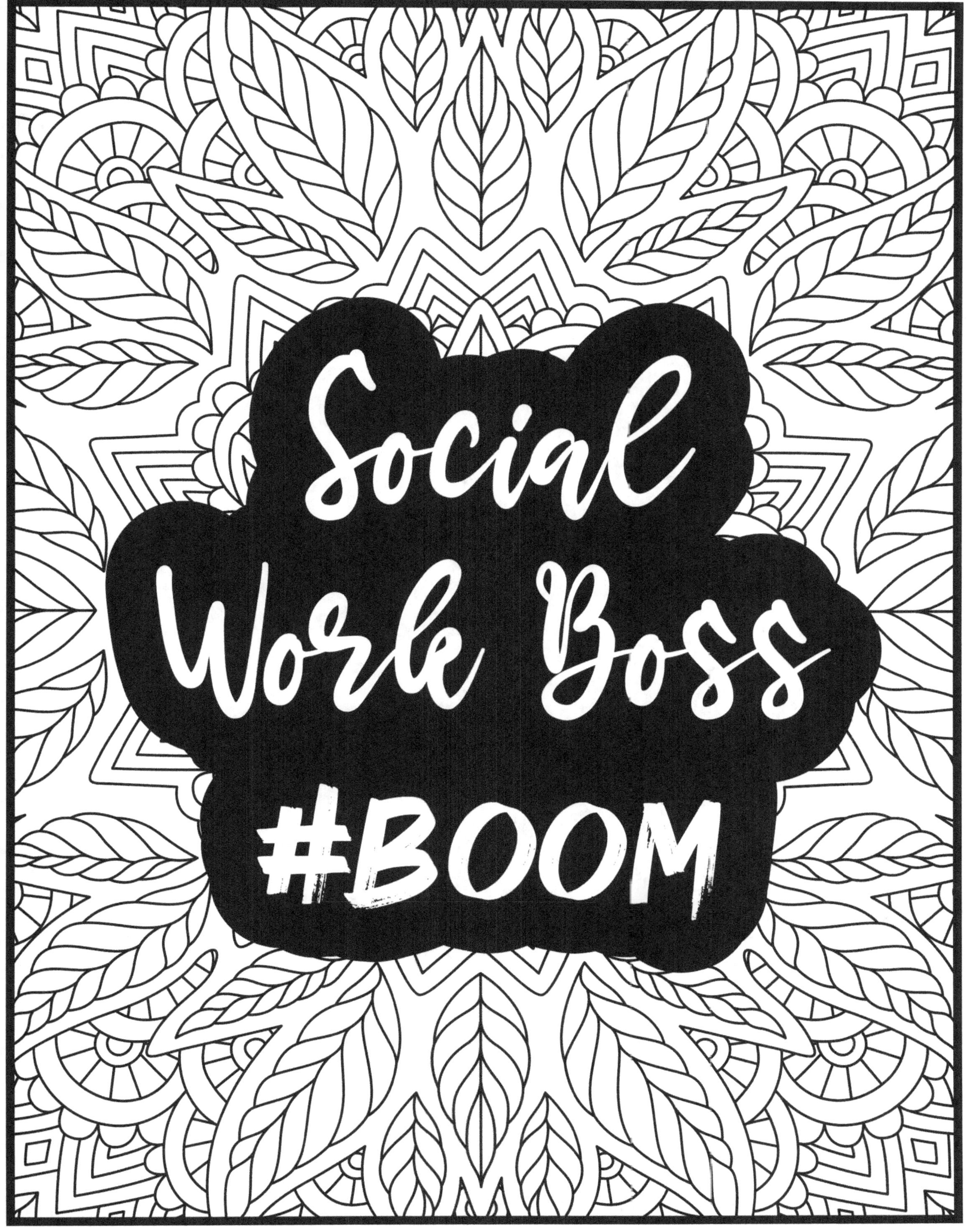

Social
Work Boss
#BOOM

Bouncing forward,
not backwards.
#RESILIENCE

15

I'm not putting
Out this
Fire today.
#LetItBurn

16

Challenging the norm.
#DISRUPTOR

17

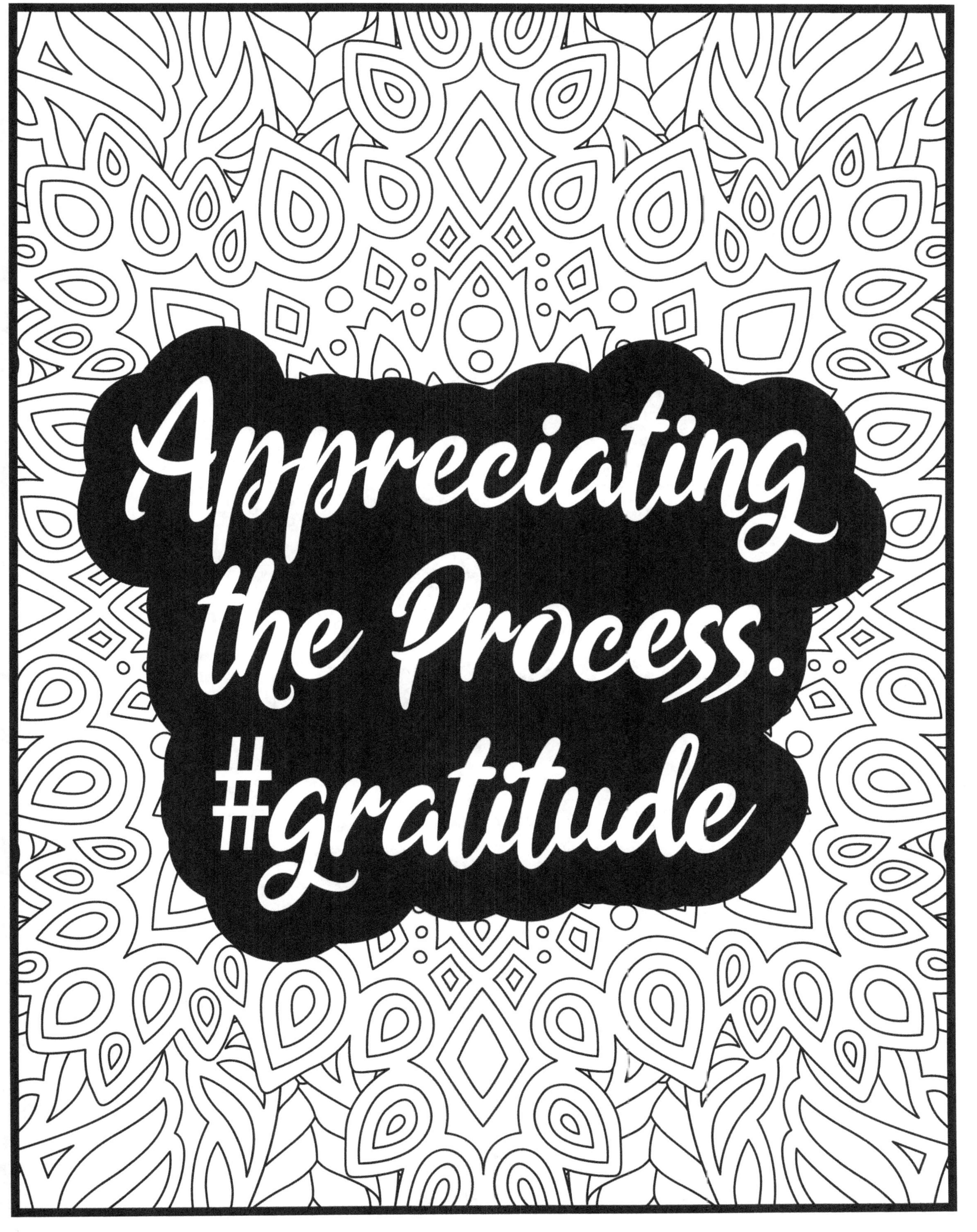

Appreciating
the Process.
#gratitude

18

Whew!
#justBREATHE

Super Social Worker! #yep

20

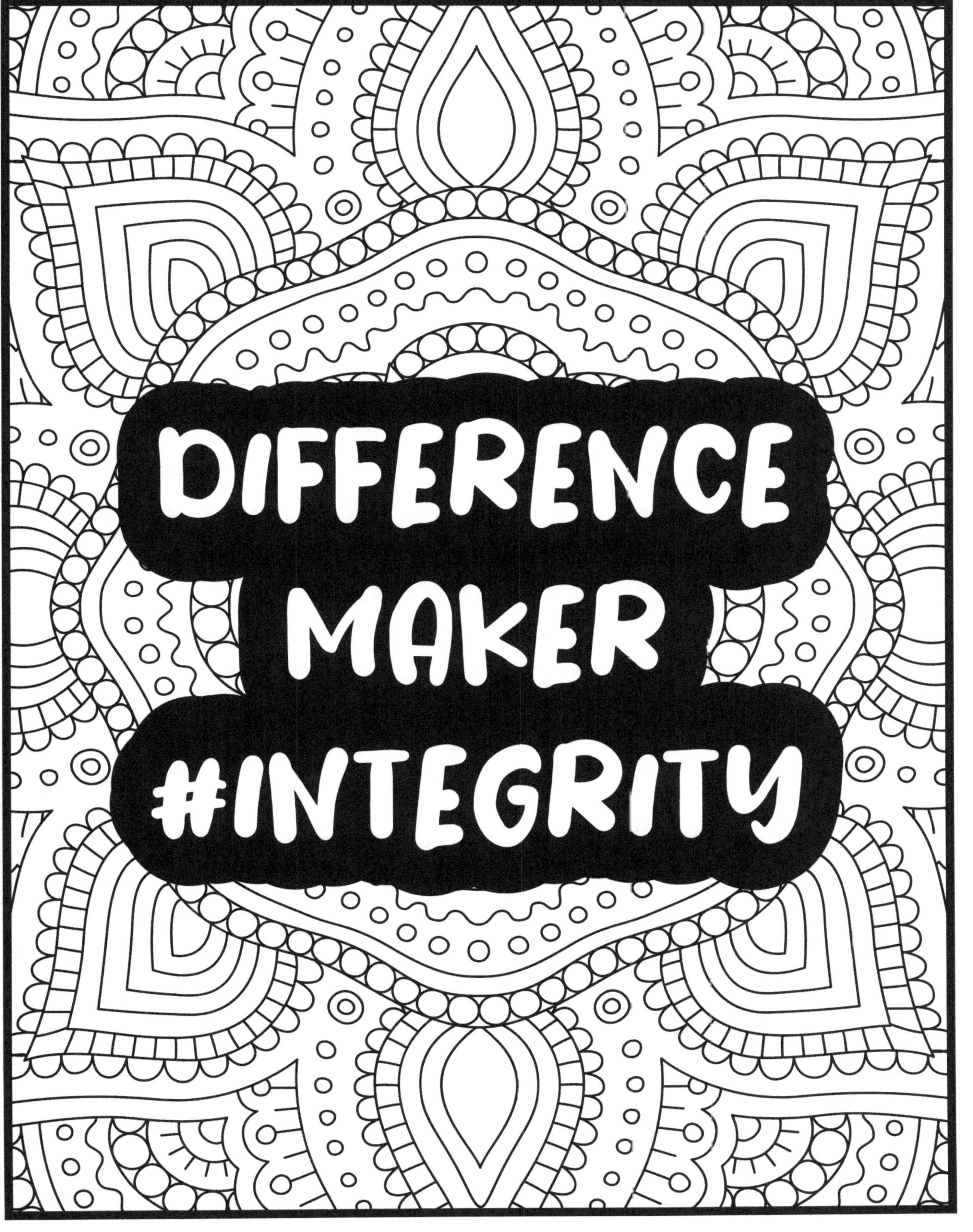

DIFFERENCE
MAKER
#INTEGRITY

21

Saving the world
one treatment
goal at a time.
#socialwork

22

Certified Chaos
Coordinator
#INeedaVacay

23

Licensed
Problem Solver.
#SkilledSocialWorker

LETTING GO OF THE THINGS I CAN'T CONTROL. #PURSUEPEACE

25

Tooting my
Own horn today!
#SelfAppreciation

NO EXPLANATION NEEDED.
#BOUNDARIES

27

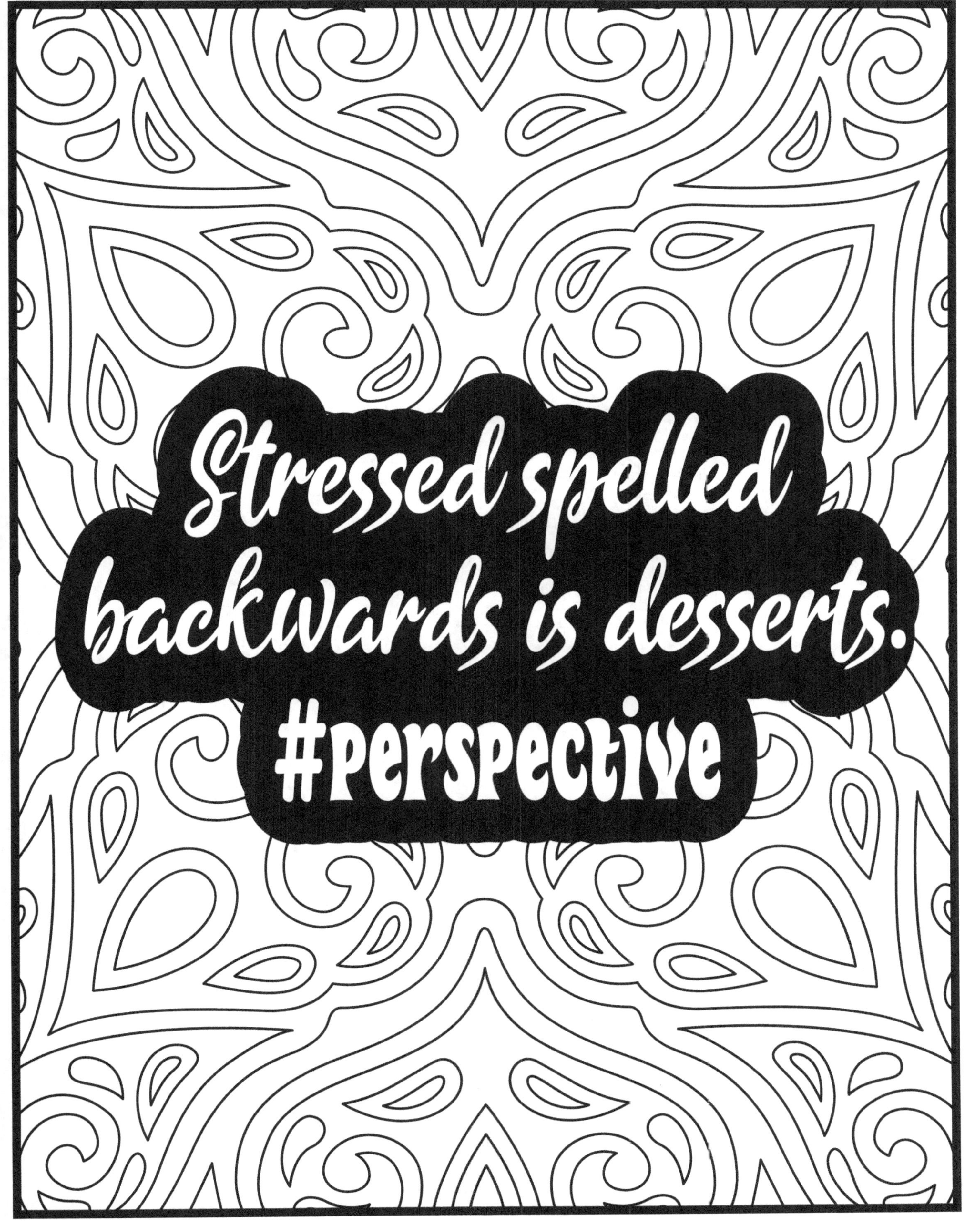
Stressed spelled backwards is desserts.
#perspective

28

NO IS A
COMPLETE SENTENCE.
#BOUNDARIES

29

No excuses.
#GetItDone

DEAR STRESS,
NOT TODAY!
#STRESSMANAGEMENT

31

Proceed
with caution.
#You'veBeenWarned

32

THERE WILL BE
NO CRISIS
TODAY.
#BOOKED&BUSY

33

I skipped the meeting to actually do some work. #productivity

34

IT'S HANDLED!
#LikeABoss

35

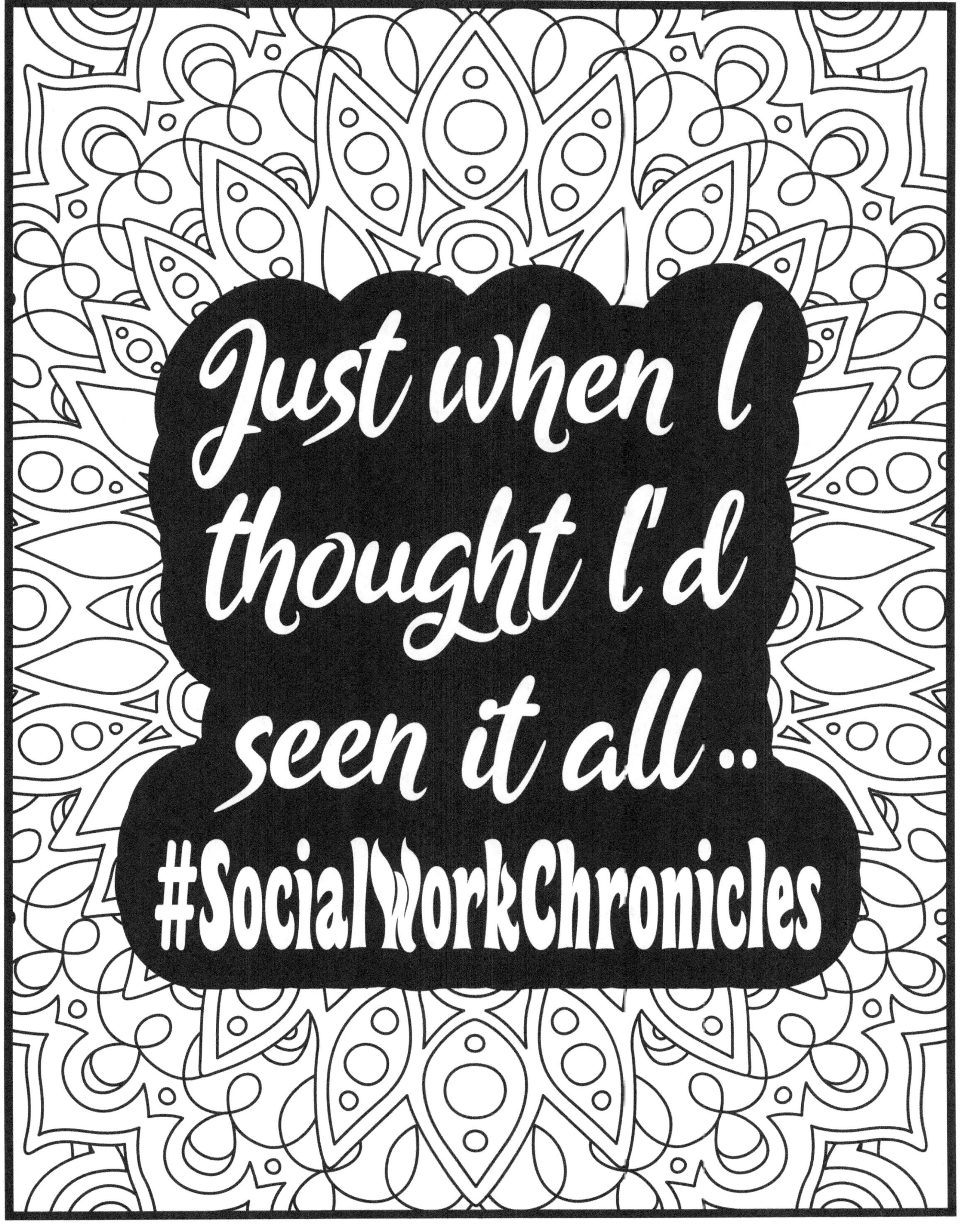

Just when I thought I'd seen it all...
#SocialWorkChronicles

36

Today is
MY Friday!
#TGIF

If you can send
It in an email
Don't have the
Meeting.
#Meetingetiquette101

NO STRESS
ZONE
#NOSTRESSALLOWED

I'm not
Procrastinating,
I'm self-caring!
#Unplug

40

THOU SHALL NOT TRY ME TODAY!
#NOTANYDAY

41

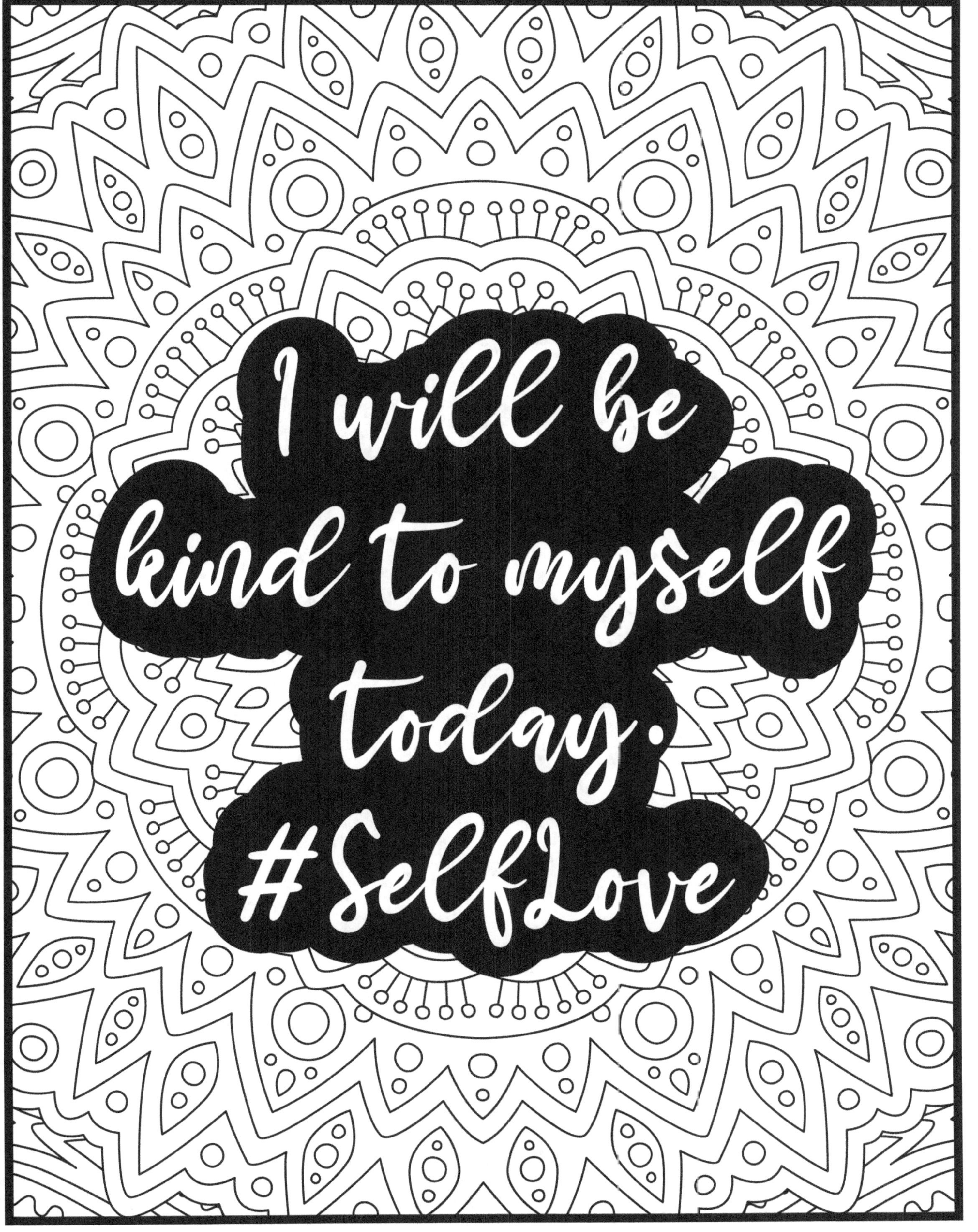

I will be kind to myself today. #SelfLove

42

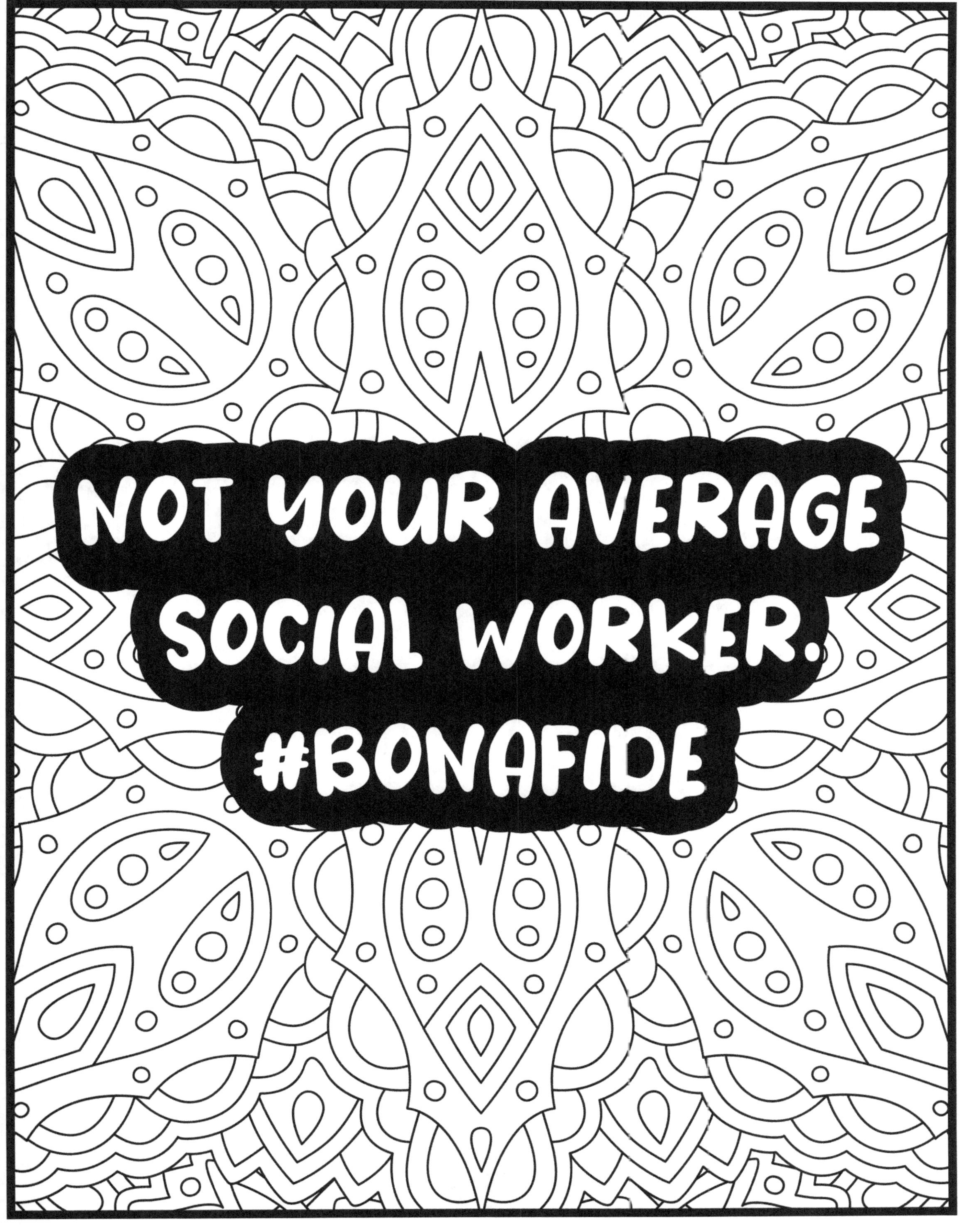

NOT YOUR AVERAGE SOCIAL WORKER.
#BONAFIDE

43

SELF-CARE
ME, PLEASE!
#RIGHTNOW

44

ABOUT THE AUTHOR

Terricka Hardy, LCSW, ACSW, BCD is a Subject Matter Expert in Self-Care and Resilience. Terricka Hardy is a Licensed Clinical Social Worker, member of the Academy of Certified Social Workers, Board Certified Diplomate on Clinical Social Work, and Certified Compassion Fatigue Professional. She is an appointed member of the National Association of Social Workers (NASW) National Ethics Committee and member of the Editorial Board for the Journal for Social Work Values and Ethics. Terricka is the owner of Terricka Hardy Consulting, LLC and has trained numerous of organizations, professionals, and community groups in ethics, mental health, burnout, self-care, and resilience. Terricka has presented and trained numerous of professionals both nationally and internationally. She is the author of the Self-Care A-Z Adult Coloring Book , Work Perks: A Gratitude Journal for Helping Professionals, and the Color Out Loud ™ Adult Coloring Book Series all available on Amazon.

Contact Terricka for your staff training needs or to speak at your next event at thardylcsw@yahoo.com
For bulk book orders please contact thardylcsw@yahoo.com

CONTACT:
Email: thardylcsw@yahoo.com
Facebook: Terricka Hardy, LCSW
LinkedIn: Terricka Hardy
Website: www.terrickahardy.com

Share your beautiful and creative coloring pages, from this book, with the author by emailing a picture of your work to thardylcsw@yahoo.com.